AF477632

HOW TO BECOME A SUPER-SALESMAN

A short and simple course in the Science of Salesmanship. Based upon a lifetime of study and practical experience. Teaching the One Great Fact of human nature, an exact knowledge of which has enabled the world's greatest salesmen, organizers, executives, leaders, commanders, reformers, preachers, orators, geniuses and statesmen to make people believe what they wanted them to believe and act as they wanted them to act. An effective method of influencing, persuading, handling and controlling people, individually and collectively, in personal relations, business, social life, politics, court practice, and the pulpit and especially in professional salesmanship and advertising.

By ARTHUR NEWCOMB

Rescued from the archives of the 1920's by David Hoffman
With a Foreword for today's peddlers by Kristi Witker

American Heritage Press New York

Published in Canada by Fitzhenry & Whiteside.
Library of Congress Catalogue Card Number: 75-117359
SBN: 8281-0109-4

FOREWORD

This book can change your life, reader. Do not scorn it. Do you feel that the universe is a superconspiracy to put you down? Do you feel, as you inch toward the office, redigesting your predigested breakfast food and inhaling clouds of exhaust gas, that perhaps you aren't getting anywhere? Rejoice. The author of this half-century-old guide has the answers for you. Becoming a supersalesman is only part of what he promises as a result of his course. Learn to read faces as he teaches and—without laying out an extra dollar for a new hair cream, toothpaste, or cologne—you can acquire instant power over others. You can manipulate your way to power, money, sex. Mafiosi will beg you to allow their lawyers to do your tax returns. Beautiful movie stars will bribe your employer to be hired as your secretary. Manly athletes will fight back tears of gratitude if you nod to them from your free box seat.

You will, of course, encounter some problems. Let them be a challenge to you. Reading faces is not as easy as it was fifty years back. For one thing, the prominent chin, the short upper lip, the ruddy cheek, and other telltale signs of character are now all too often disguised by sideburns, beards, and other appendages of the hirsute. It is sad that we no longer live in the honest era of Warren G. Harding, when men were barefaced and businesslike. Today the bare face is the rare face. Can we wonder at our degeneration when the contact lens, the toupee, the padded shoulder invite us to deceitfulness? Still, the diligent and dedicated observer can penetrate the camouflage imposed by the barber, the cosmetician, the orthodontist, and the plastic surgeon—*if* he is armed with this book.

The perceptive reader will note that most of the faces herein illustrated are male. So many women are in business today—a change from a half-century ago—that this is a serious omission. Yet a catalogue of female physiognomies might prove useless. Women are showing so many more interesting things these days that is is a rare man who notices their faces.

The bright lad who wants to get ahead in a business organization where women play important roles may have to devise other strategies.

Writing fifty years ago, the author was also quite naturally unaware of some instincts that have appeared in recent years and of their identifying signs. Two examples are the Instinct To Use the Expense Account (immediately revealed by the calloused thumb and index finger used in presenting the company credit card) and the Instinct To Do Everything by Phone. Those with the latter instinct can be spotted by circular dents in their ears, which are also usually flattened and enlarged.

The basic principles, however, remain sound. Before applying them to your wife, supervisor, or banker, practice by analyzing photographs of distinguished Americans. You will note that the author of this book brilliantly creates portraits of Herbert Hoover (Figure 19), F. D. R. (Figure 20), and Calvin Coolidge (Figure 23) simply by combining the features of different personality types. See if you can reverse the process by describing the inner dynamics of (a) Spiro Agnew, (b) Dale Carnegie, (c) Tiny Tim, (d) Eddie Gilbert, (e) all of the above, from their portraits. GOOD LUCK, and may happiness, power, and higher tax brackets be yours.

—Kristi Witker

How to Become a Supersalesman

HOW TO SIZE PEOPLE UP

John Wallace stepped into the private office of President Harris of the Bigtown Gas Company by appointment.

He wanted to sell the company several hundred thousand dollars' worth of health, accident, old-age and life insurance for its ten thousand employees.

He had spent weeks preparing a talk showing how greatly the company would profit by keeping its employees loyal, steady, free from worry and more permanent in their jobs.

He took one look at President Harris, whom he had not seen before.

Then he threw overboard every word of his carefully prepared talk.

Instead he told a simple story, about a little girl whose father was ill for a year before he died, and how that little girl had to give up school to go to work. He then painted a glowing word-picture of what she might have become if her father had been properly insured.

Then he said, "Mr. Harris, there are thousands of little girls in the families of your employees who may have the same experiences—hundreds, certainly, who will go through such sorrows and dangers—unless you adopt a modern and scientific form of insurance for their sake.

"You have had experience enough with your employees to know that every penny you spend for them in any such way as this comes back to you ten-fold, although you know, and I know, that you do not do it for that reason."

After that it was a mere question of settling the details of the insurance plan and signing the contract.

John Wallace knew what he was doing when he changed his entire plan and threw aside his talk that had cost him weeks of work and a good deal of money.

He did not guess.

He did not merely "follow a hunch," and take a chance.

He knew, as well as if he had read it on a sign in letters a foot high, that President Harris was a man of high ideals, keen sympathies, great natural benevolence, a passion for protecting and providing for the weak and the helpless, and almost maternal love of children.

He saw too that, while President Harris had been a great money maker, and was naturally interested in the game of making money, he had now reached the point where he had all the money he needed and felt very much deeper and more personal interest in philanthropic and benevolent plans—especially for those who he felt were under his protection and control.

John Wallace knew these things because he knew what any man was, at heart and in character, by looking at him.

There was nothing uncanny about this.

It was not a peculiar personal gift that John Wallace had.

You Already Know How to Size People Up

You have just as much natural gift for knowing what people are by looking at them as John Wallace had.

You *do* know what people are, to a certain extent, by looking at them.

You do size people up every time you meet them.

You know the hearty, genial, friendly, good fellow from the narrow-minded, hard, dyspeptic grouch.

You know the bragging, bluffing, cowardly bully from the fine, gentle, sensitive but courageous man.

You know the shrewd, keen, alert, hard-headed, practical man from the credulous, over-confident dreamer and theorist.

You can tell what these people are by looking at them, even by looking at their photographs.

You may possibly know all of these differences in men, in their looks, and a good many more without knowing exactly how you know.

John Wallace not only knew but knew how he knew, and so could always be sure.

The Science of Character Analysis

Now the whole question of the differences among people, the differences in their looks, and the correspondence between traits of character and certain outward appearance, has been reduced very nearly if not quite to a science.

It is not infallible. You or I may make mistakes in applying it, just as a physician may make a mistake in applying his knowledge of diagnosis and medicine. Yet it is accurate enough, and dependable enough, so that thousands of salesmen, employers, and others are using it constantly in their daily work and finding it worth while.

In studying these various types you will discover that all people have a certain development of all of the instincts and desires;

That in some people certain instincts and desires are more strongly developed, and exercise a greater power over thought, speech and action than others;

That sometimes one instinct, or one desire, may very greatly overbalance and overshadow all the rest;

That in other cases two or more instincts or desires may predominate;

That in still other cases there may be a very fair degree of balance among all the instincts and desires.

Making Combinations.—The lesson for you in these conclusions is that you cannot afford to judge any person by any one indication alone, but must take everything about that person into consideration in forming your conclusions.

For example, if you find that a man has all the indications of a very strong instinct for combat and at the same time all the indications of a passionate desire to serve others, what would be your conclusion about him?

Simply that he would express his desire to serve others by fighting for them, by fighting for his ideals, for the uplift of humanity.

Suppose, on the other hand, that the man with every indication of a strong instinct for combat also showed every indication of a strong instinct for possession.

Then, naturally enough, he would enter with all his heart into the contest for business—the game of making money.

In a similar way you form your conclusions as to the effect of any other combination of instincts.

I can only give you a start here in the wonderfully fascinating and valuable science and art of sizing people up.

The more you observe people, the more you study them, the more you apply what you learn here, the more you add to this knowledge by your own observations, the easier it will become for you to size people up accurately.

Figure 1—Instinct for Life.

How to Appeal to This Man

Emphasize safety, health, sanitation, longevity, and, by analogy, security, provision for future, and precaution against loss.

Instinct for Life

Self-preservation has been said to be the first law of nature.

There is, and has been some dispute about this.

However that may be, it is certain enough that some people have a very much keener instinct for self-preservation than others; that some people cling to life much more tenaciously than others; that some people are very much more cautious and prudent about keeping themselves alive and healthy than others; that some people are very much more courageous and determined in fighting disease, discouragement, difficulties, disappointments, weariness and death than others.

Those in whom the instinct for life has power have wide heads. Compare the head on page 12 with that shown on page 52 and you will quickly see the difference.

The individual who has keen instinct for the preservation of life, and usually lives long, also has a large nose, high in the bridge, indicating good lung capacity and active use of the lungs.

His ears are also large and usually long rather than wide, with large, full lobes.

These people usually have long rather than round faces, due to the fact that the chin is usually long and rather square.

The upper lip, also, is usually long rather than short, while the head presents a square appearance at the top as seen from the back.

In body-build these people usually have long trunks, rather full, well-developed chests, comparatively small waists, and short, sturdy arms and legs.

The long trunk seems to give plenty of room for the proper functioning of the vital organs, while the short arms and legs would seem to indicate that the vital organs are large and competent compared with the bony and muscular frame they have to support and sustain.

These people are cautious, conservative, do not take chances, but are watchful and prudent.

They are inclined to make provision for the future, to be independent and self-reliant by nature.

They love activity, travel and motion, but are deliberate, cautious and moderate in their expenditure of energy.

They are industrious and usually constant in their work rather than spasmodic, impatient and fretful.

These people not only love life for themselves but they love the life around them; so they are usually kindly, thoughtful, interested in people, and nearly always optimistic and cheerful.

Figure 2—Instinct for Food.

How to Appeal to This Man

Let him actually see, smell, taste, and handle things good to eat, drink, smoke, and enjoy.

Describe enjoyable food or the enjoyment of food. It takes money to buy food, so show him how he can make a profit. Appeal to his love of ease and comfort and his preference for executive or administrative work.

Instinct for Food

People with whom the instinct for food is very strong are very easily recognized.

Their necks are usually thick, the distance from the opening of the ear to the back of the neck is long, and the lower part of the back of the head is full and round.

These people are interested in good things to eat, good things to drink, and in the good things and comforts of life generally.

Occasionally you will see a slender person with a narrow head and collapsed cheeks who has full red lips and a rather voracious appetite.

This man's digestion is like a coarse sieve. He has to eat a great deal because only a little of what he eats is really digested and assimilated. He has rather an abnormal development of the instinct for food, but his instinct as to what is really good to eat is not nearly so sure and correct as that of the fat man.

It is not a good idea to talk business with people of this type when they are hungry.

They usually can be very much more easily persuaded after they have had a good meal.

If you are entertaining people of this type feed them well.

If you want to appeal to their sympathy tell them about people who lack food.

Figure 3—Instinct for Comfortable Temperature.

How to Appeal to This Man

Let him feel (or describe to him) softness, fineness, and warmth of clothing for winter; lightness, sheerness, and coolness of clothing for summer.

The same principle applies to radiators, furnaces, stoves, building materials, electric fans, shade trees, awnings, hammocks, motor cars, motor boats, winter resorts, summer resorts, and climate in general.

Instinct for Comfortable Temperature

People of dark, or brunet color, are much more sensitive to temperature, as a general rule, than people of light or blond color. They are of course much more sensitive to cold than to heat, whereas, as a general rule the blond is more sensitive to heat than to cold. The blond is, however, particularly sensitive to bright sunlight.

It is very difficult for these people to undergo hardships of any kind.

They can be depended upon to respond readily to any appeal to their instinct for comfort and luxury.

Roughing it or pioneering does not appeal strongly to these people. They want all the modern improvements, conveniences and comforts.

Figure 4—Instinct for Physical Activity.

How to Appeal to This Man

In bringing a prospect of this type to decision and action, bear in mind his love of liberty and his desire for independence and freedom. Make him feel he is making the decision for himself and on his own initiative.

The Instinct for Physical Activity

One of the most important classifications of human beings is that based upon the instinct for physical activity.

The strongest possible indications of this instinct are: Blond color; head wide above and slightly in front of the ears; high cheek bones; high bridge of nose; square jaws; broad, square shoulders; deep chest; large bones and muscles; large, square, elastic hands; large feet, and either a long rangy build, or a short stocky one, both without undue slenderness or great stoutness.

These people not only love physical activity, but are fond of motion, machinery, construction, transportation, military and naval service, all kinds of outdoor sports and games.

They are usually independent, liberty-loving, demanding large scope for their activities, impatient of restraint and confinement, and devoted to political, religious and civic freedom as well as physical.

In the lower grades this type of people do the actual manual labor of the world.

In the higher grades, where more mentality is developed, they are engineers, pioneers, executives, inventors, salesmen, contractors, generals, admirals, and in general do some form of mental work in connection with building, construction, transportation, manufacturing and military and naval affairs.

Savonarola, Cromwell, Gladstone, Lincoln, Grant, Roosevelt and Wilson and many others distinguished for their labor in the cause of human liberty have been men of this type or modifications of it.

Figure 5—Instinct for Rest and Sleep.

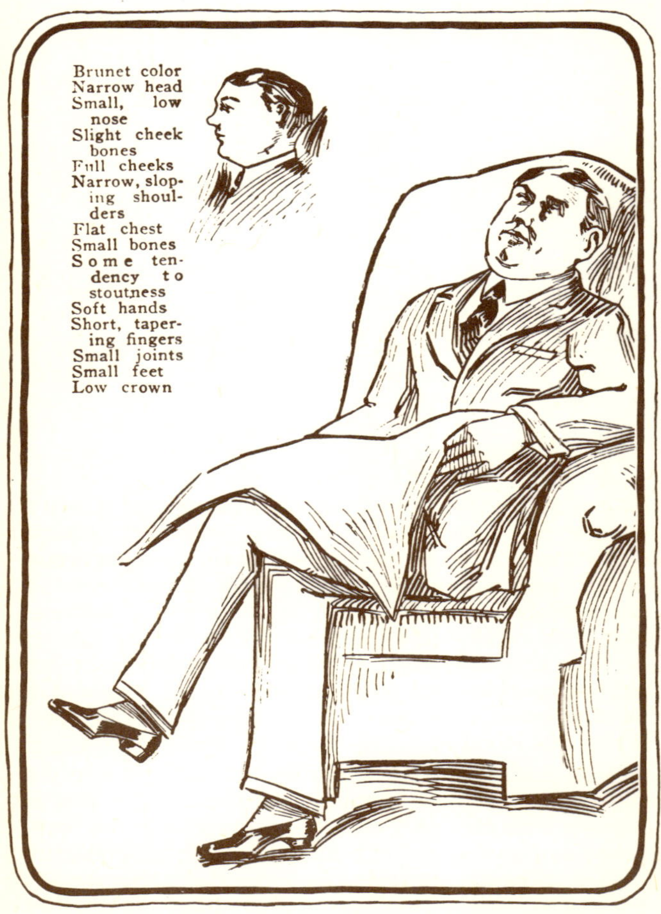

How to Appeal to This Man

This type loves ease and comfort. Show him how your proposition will add to his comfort and desire for rest. Show him a picture of himself enjoying the advantages you offer.

Instinct for Rest and Sleep

The instinct for rest and sleep after periods of activity exists in every human being. Some, however, require more rest than others; some are naturally less energetic and better satisfied with simple inactivity than others.

Most human beings require some manner of self-expression, either physical or mental.

The man who demands physical activity has been described and pictured on pages 18 and 19.

The man who demands mental activity will be pictured and described on pages 22 and 23.

The heads of many of these individuals are low in the crown, or at the point just above the ears. If this is much lower than the head just above and behind the forehead they are unreasonably optimistic, hopeful, cheerful, imaginative, dreamy, believers in luck, and always waiting for something to turn up to their advantage rather than hustling to gain advantage by their own efforts.

These are the procrastinators—the people who are always *going to do* something brilliant.

If indulged and supplied with means by others, they are quite likely to become professional invalids.

Figure 6—Instinct for Mental Activity.

How to Appeal to This Man

This man likes to learn, to know facts and reasons, to improve his mind. He is interested in education, literature, science, philosophy, and intellectual matters generally. Appeal to his desire to learn and his preference for intellectual work.

Instinct for Mental Activity

There are people who do not care greatly for physical activity, who do not have the necessary physical equipment for it, but who have very active brains and nervous systems and cannot endure mental inactivity.

These people are eager for knowledge, usually studious, great planners and schemers, research workers, teachers, writers, lecturers, philosophers, scientists, artists and others who do the strictly intellectual work of the world.

In the lower grades they are clerks, stenographers, bookkeepers, retail salesmen and saleswomen, milliners, dressmakers and, in general, workers on fine, delicate materials, requiring high finish, great accuracy or artistic excellence.

They do not like, and are not fitted for, hard manual labor, they cannot endure rough, crude, coarse, uncomfortable, grimy or ugly surroundings and are usually sensitive and responsive.

Figure 7—Instinct for Combat.

How to Appeal to This Man

Use the law of non-resistance. Do not quarrel or fight with him unless you want to finish the job and thoroughly conquer him. He often respects the man who has whipped him. Appeal to his love of conquest. Show him how your proposition will help him win—how it will enable him to out-distance competition.

Instinct for Combat

Pugnacity, or the instinct for combat, is universal in all forms of life. Like all other instincts, however, it is very much stronger in some individuals than in others.

This type of man is the aggressive fighter.

Many other types of men fight well on the defensive, but in them the instinct for combat is not so strong as in the aggressive fighter.

This type of man carries his instinct for combat not only into actual physical battle, but into every field of human endeavor and interest.

He is fond of conquest. He likes to win, whether in love, social affairs, business, in sports and games, in politics, in all matters of argument and opinion, and in all matters relating to personal dignity, authority and prestige.

These people, therefore, are courageous, aggressive, direct, forceful and dynamic.

This instinct for combat is therefore a very large part of the desire for superiority, and shows itself in every activity of man in which he strives to show himself superior to his fellows, or to have himself considered in any way superior to his fellows.

Figure 8—Instinct for Sex.

How to Appeal to This Man

Those in whom this instinct shows strongly are full of life, vigor, zest, and courage. They are interested in those of the opposite sex. Their desire to be attractive can always be appealed to successfully, provided your appeal is fitted to the degree of refinement and moral caliber of the individual.

Instinct for Sex

Instinct for sex in human beings is greatly diversified and complicated. In some it is almost entirely a spiritual, aesthetic quality; in others it is almost entirely a gross, sensual, physical quality.

It is, therefore, difficult to give all of the indications of a strong sex instinct.

These people often have tapering hands and fingers, and show their sex instinct by coquettishness, vivacity, energy and ambition.

People who are deficient in the sex instinct are usually pale, colorless, thin-lipped, small at the base of the brain and are deficient in energy, sparkle, wit, courage, enthusiasm, personal charm.

Figure 9—Instinct for Companionship.

How to Appeal to This Man

Make friends with this man. Put your dealings with him on a basis of friendship. Appeal to his desire to be with his friends, to please them, and to serve them. Also appeal to his love of home and family, especially if he is a brunet. You may also appeal to his love of flowers and pets.

Instinct for Companionship

The human being is naturally gregarious. That is, he enjoys the society of his own kind.

There are many different expressions of this instinct, and many different degrees of it in different kinds of people.

Those of blond color usually like crowds, gaiety, excitement, a wide circle of acquaintances rather than a very small circle of intimate friends.

Those of brunet color are more quiet, more fond of nature, home, the garden, more affectionate with the members of their families, fonder of pets, and much more inclined to associate themselves with a small circle of intimate friends rather than a large circle of acquaintances.

People who particularly love companionship with others usually have a friendly, genial, alert expression.

Those who are deficient in this respect oftentimes have either a cold, stern, forbidding expression or a remote, dreamy, absent-minded, philosophical look, which indicates that they prefer the companionship of their own thoughts to conversation with others.

There are people who utterly lack the instinct for friendship. They associate with other people only to take advantage of them. They have little or no conception of the qualities of gratitude or loyalty.

Such people are not wholly normal. They are anti-social.

One of the best places to look for a large development of the instinct for companionship is the back of the head.

When this is full, round, long from the opening of the ears back to the middle of the back head, you can be practically sure that you have to deal with a person who is very fond of people—who likes to be with them, to deal with them, to work with them, to meet and associate with them, to sell to them and to serve them.

This is the best type for development of salesmanship, advertising, law, politics, social service, the ministry, and in fact any other trade or profession, success in which depends upon success in handling, convincing and persuading people.

This is therefore the best type of back-head for the supersalesman.

Figure 10—Instinct for Possession.

How to Appeal to This Man

Show him how your proposition will help him to make money or to secure other valuable possessions.

Instinct for Possession

Instinct for possession, like most of the other instincts, takes many different and interesting forms.

One man tries to possess only things of immediate, practical utility, another to possess things of no utility—or very small utility—and great sentimental value.

One man strives, and toils, and struggles to possess something and the moment it comes into his possession loses interest in it. Another man hates the struggle of acquiring things, but clings tenaciously to what few possessions he has.

One man piles up and spreads wide his possessions, adding more and more, but pays little attention to the development and improvement of what he has.

Another man cares nothing for expansion, but tries to improve and increase the value of what he already has.

Other things being equal the blond loves to get possession—he loves the game of conquest, he loves to take the aggressive, to go pioneering, to expand, to extend his borders. He enjoys material possessions, useful possessions, practical possessions.

On the other hand the brunet is more inclined to sentimental and artistic possessions. He is not so expansive in his ideas, but he is more inclined to improve and develop what he has. He loves things for their beauty, for their excellence and for their sentimental and historical association.

In the same way the man with a wide head, especially a head wide through the temples, is aggressive and eager to acquire possessions. He is interested in money making, in buying and selling and in profits.

On the other hand the man whose head is narrow in this region is usually moderate or deficient in commercial and financial sense. He is not so much interested in money, and especially in money making.

He shows his lack of a sense of values by keeping things which have no value or little value, stowing them away, refusing to dispose of them or destroy them. They clutter up his attic, his store room, his desk and other places.

The man who is eager for possessions and keen about money making usually has shrewd eyes, not too widely open, and has a keen, alert, rather calculating expression.

The man with very widely opened eyes—so widely opened that they are almost round—is usually credulous, too confiding and too lacking in shrewdness and determination.

Figure 11—Instinct of Curiosity.

How to Appeal to This Man

Tell him, or suggest to him, enough about your proposition to make him want to know more. Show him a little so that he will want to see more. Show him, if possible, how your proposition will enable him to see interesting things or acquire secret information.

Instinct of Curiosity

The instinct of curiosity is universal. It is not only in men but also in many animals.

So strong is this instinct in almost all human beings that it is of the highest possible use in securing sufficient belief in yourself, and your proposition, to make your prospect willing to listen to you.

The first thing you say to your prospect may be something new and startling which tells him just enough about your proposition to make him want to know more.

Those in whom curiosity is very strong have arched eyebrows and an alert, wakeful, inquiring expression of the eyes and face.

A rather sharp, pointed nose, turned up at the tip, is very often found in people who are so curious as to be what is generally termed "nosey." They want to know everything that is going on, and especially do they want to know all they can find out about people around them.

Some people are intensely curious along some one line, and not so much curious about other things.

For example, a man whose instinct for food is strong will be eager for knowledge about good things to eat. A man whose instinct for physical activity is strong will be curious about athletic records, automobiles, flying machines and other things that appeal to his desire for motion and machinery.

One of the best ways to arouse the interest of a prospect who is beginning to show signs of indifference and mind wandering is to tell him something or ask him something which will arouse his curiosity.

Figure 12—Desire for Shelter and Clothing.

How to Appeal to This Type

Appeal to the particular form or forms of this desire, as indicated above and in the text. Do not make the mistake of trying to sell an elaborate, richly ornamented garment or house to one who desires only durability and utility. Do not try to sell a coarse, crude, or cheap product to a person with very fine skin, hair, and features.

Desire for Shelter and Clothing

People desire shelter and clothing for so many different reasons and have such widely different tastes in regard to them, that a rather extended consideration of the indications of this desire in human beings is advisable.

The individual with coarse hair, coarse skin, large rugged features, large joints and large hands and feet is usually more interested in bulk and size, in strength and massiveness than in high finish and beauty.

He is usually satisfied with coarse-textured materials, and rather coarse and crude furnishings.

If he is eager to be noticed and to make a display, he usually is inclined to extreme styles, bright colors and over-ornamentation.

The individual with fine hair, fine skin, finely-chiseled features, slender bones, small hands and feet, likes fine-textured clothing, beautiful surroundings, artistic finish, quality rather than quantity. He is more interested in beauty than in mere gaudy display. Eyes set wide apart, with rather full, well-formed brows, indicate a natural sense of the beautiful in line and proportion.

The individual with a short upper lip, which easily rises when the individual smiles and displays the upper teeth, usually likes to be conspicuous, likes display, is interested in the beauty, style, finish and decoration of his home and of his person.

The short upper lip with coarse texture indicates a desire for brilliant colors, over-decoration, an abundance of jewelry, ribbons, laces and furbelows on the dress, and a very ornate style of architecture in the home, with lavishness of display.

People with hard hands want durable clothing, durable furniture and a general air of plainness, severity and durability in their homes in general.

People with soft hands like soft, comfortable things and flimsy things. They are subject to frequent changes in their tastes and can never be depended upon to like any one particular thing, or kind of thing, long at a time.

In general, people of blond coloring select their homes and clothing for the sake of display and entertainment. This, of course, is often modified by other considerations as stated above.

Brunet people usually prefer quiet, domestic homes with provisions for the family and intimate friends rather than for larger gatherings of guests.

Figure 13—Desire for Pleasure.

How to Appeal to This Man

Let him actually enjoy some favorite form of pleasure in your proposition, if possible; if not, paint a vivid mental picture of him enjoying such pleasure in, with, or as a result of your proposition.

Desire for Pleasure

In the broadest sense of the word the desire for pleasure is strong in every human being. The differences among them are, in reality, their differences in the way they seek and find their pleasures.

In a more restricted sense "pleasure" is usually used to designate the more relaxing forms of amusement, such as dances, parties, theatres, athletic contests where the pleasure seekers are mere spectators, automobiling, traveling, yachting, social dinners, suppers, luncheons and what are sometimes called "frivolities" in general.

These forms of pleasure are more frequently enjoyed by blonds than by brunets. The blond enjoys gayety, the lights and crowds; while the brunet is more likely to find his pleasures at home, in his garden, among his trees, in the enjoyment of nature and the rather close association with family, friends and pets.

People with retreating foreheads, prominent brows, prominent eyes, large prominent noses, prominent mouths and retreating chins are usually very much more interested in active participation in the pleasures they enjoy. People with prominent upper foreheads, flat brows, retreating eyes, small noses, retreating mouths and chins prominent at the point are more inclined to quiet pleasures and to enjoyment as spectators.

The high, broad forehead with fine-textured hair, skin, features, hands and feet, usually indicates pleasure in reading, in lectures, in drama, in concerts and generally in what are called the "highbrow" or "fine-haired" kinds of pleasure and recreation. People of this type, who are also athletic in build, will seek pleasures in outdoor sports, tramping, canoeing, boating or motoring.

Oftentimes crisp, wavy hair—especially when associated with tapering hands and fingers—indicates artistic appreciation. You may expect a person with those marks to seek his pleasures in concerts, operas, the theatre, art galleries or some other such interest.

Square jaw, square shoulders, large hands and feet, large bones and muscles, always indicate a natural desire for active pleasures in the open.

People who have coarse hair, coarse skin, rugged features and are rather crudely built are inclined to enjoy the more vigorous, virile, vivid, coarse and crude pleasures.

Figure 14—Desire for Superiority.

How to Appeal to This Man

If he is coarse in texture and not naturally dignified or suspicious, flatter him openly, but justly. If he is fine, or naturally dignified, or suspicious, be more tactful in your praise. Then show him how your proposition will help him to attract attention, to be admired, praised, and envied. Paint a mental picture of him enjoying the superiority or applause he would gain through your proposition.

Desire for Superiority

Desire for superiority takes on as many forms and leads in as many directions as the desire for pleasure.

Some men desire to be, or to appear to be, superior to all others in goodness, justice, kindness, generosity and morality. Other men take the exact opposite and seem to desire to be, or appear to be, superior to all others in meanness, wickedness and crime.

This second desire, however, is not normal, but is a mark of insanity, degeneracy or perversion.

Generally speaking, those of blond coloring desire conquest, authority, position and influence.

The brunet, on the other hand, tries to excel in religion, in scholarship, in philosophy, in artistic excellence.

It is natural, therefore, for the blond to wish to excel and be superior in the eyes of the crowd while the brunet is more inclined to want to excel and be superior in his own regard and in the eyes of his family and intimate friends.

As you might expect, the man who is all brains and only slightly developed physically has a natural desire to excel in mental capacities and mental achievements.

The bony and muscular man with a square jaw likes to excel in athletic sports, to win games and contests of that kind.

A man with fine hair, fine skin and finely chiseled features is sensitive to criticism, has a great love of refinement, culture and beauty. His natural tendency, therefore, will be to desire superiority in refinement, in culture, in the beauty of his clothing, his home, his furnishings and surroundings and superior knowledge in music, art, letters or some other form of culture.

The man whose head is high, especially from the opening of the ears vertically upward, desires superiority in rulership and authority. He loves approval and applause and is sometimes inclined to be proud.

The man whose back head is full, round and broad desires to appear well in politics, in society, in his clubs, among his friends.

The short upper lip, which so easily rises, when its possessor smiles, and displays the upper teeth, indicates a great desire for approval, for attention, for praise, for applause, for notice and for being conspicuous.

Figure 15—Desire to Serve Others.

How to Appeal to This Man

Appeal to sympathy, generosity, altruism, idealism, sense of duty, and desire to educate, improve, and uplift. Paint a vivid mental picture of the benefits some one or more people would enjoy through your proposition.

Desire for Service to Others

There are, in general, four motives which cause people to render service to others.

First, there is the purely and crudely selfish one which renders service simply for the sake of getting something in return.

Second, there is that motive for service which springs from a desire for approval. People to whom this desire is very strong, as shown by the short upper lip, are usually courteous, affable, agreeable, accommodating and try hard to give service and pleasure to others for the sake of being praised for it.

Third, there is the motive which arises very largely from idealism—a desire to serve humanity in the mass. This is oftentimes wholly unselfish and very effective. People who serve others from this motive, however, are oftentimes indifferent to individuals. Their great desire is to reform, to uplift, to make over humanity according to their high ideals.

Fourth, there is that natural, unselfish, self-effacing desire to serve others which springs from pure love. It may be the love of a parent for a child, the love of a husband for a wife or a wife for a husband, the love of a child for his parents, the love of brothers, of sisters, the love of near relatives, the love of intimate friends or the love of any human being who comes within reach.

Service to others for purely selfish ends is usually shown by a head which is low over the temples and just behind the forehead, short and straight in the back and is oftentimes accompanied by a look of shrewdness and cunning, or by servility and oiliness of demeanor.

Service to others for the sake of applause and appreciation is shown by the short upper lip.

You should have a care, however, as plenty of people with short upper lips also serve others for more noble motives.

Those who are altruistic, humanitarian, and idealistic, without being truly friendly to individuals, have a head which is high and dome-shaped above the temples, and just back of the forehead; also high and full above the ears, but short and deficient from the ears back.

Those who serve others for unselfish reasons have a head normally well developed above the temples and behind the forehead also full and round from the ears back, kindly eyes, curved and rather full lips, and true friendliness in expression of face, in handshake, and in manner.

Figure 16—Desire to Serve One's Country.

How to Appeal to This Man

Any sound and sincere appeal to patriotism will find this man responsive. He will resent, however, any attempt to commercialize his patriotism or any cheap and canting or ranting appeals.

Desire to Serve One's Country

Patriotism is so natural and normal to human beings that its absence is usually due either to abnormalities of intellect and emotion, or to grave defects in environment and education.

It is therefore rather difficult to point out anything specific which indicates an unusual degree of patriotism on the one hand, or a lack of patriotism on the other.

While this is true, you would no doubt be justified in looking for greater patriotism in a man with a high crown than in one with a low crown; in a man with a square jaw, and moderately well-developed physical organization than in an under-developed, under-nourished weakling; in a man whose head was full and round at the back, near the crown, than in a man whose head was flat at this point.

There are many different ways, of course, in which patriotism shows itself. The man who is highly intelligent, well educated, successful in business, and of an assured social position is usually rather conservative, rather moderate, rather inclined to protect and sustain things as they are, or, if he is progressive, to wish to progress by evolution, development, slowly, and cautiously.

Figure 17—Desire to Serve God.

How to Appeal to This Man

Lofty sentiments and ideals, optimism, hope, faith, worship, and religion in some form are all deeply interesting to this man and move him strongly. This is a subject, however, which must be handled with great tact. Many truly religious men resent having religion dragged into a purely business deal and are inclined to be suspicious of those who use "pious talk" in trying to make a sale.

Desire to Serve God

All people are religious, but some are more interested in religion and religious subjects than others.

The blond races have for many, many centuries been followers of some form of religion or other but, as a whole, are more interested in material things, in material progress, in organization, pioneering, construction, engineering, and empire building than in religion.

On the other hand, the brunet races are naturally religious peoples. Religion forms a large part of their thoughts, their feelings, and their lives.

It is a significant fact that the four great religions of the earth, Mohammedanism, Buddhism, Hinduism, and Christianity had their origin among brunets or dark-skinned people.

The people of India and the Orient in general are much more interested in religion, occultism, mysticism, meditation and philosophy than they are in purely material things.

The full, round, dome-shaped, top head—that is, that part of the head which is above the temples and immediately back of the forehead—is usually an indication of an interest in religious matters.

People with this type of head are either strongly religious or strongly anti-religious.

We find this type of head in Billy Sunday and Henry Ward Beecher on the one side, and in Robert G. Ingersoll on the other.

So it is not always safe to assume that because a man has this type of head he is necessarily a great churchman. He may be, on the contrary, a great agnostic. You are perfectly safe in assuming, however, that he is not indifferent to the subject of religion.

Figure 18—Quick Thought, Decision and Action.

How to Appeal to This Man

Show him—let him see—let him handle your proposition.

Give him facts—not long explanations—practical uses, not abstract theories. Show him results—actual, tangible, speedy results, if possible. Do not waste his time. Get him to act while you are with him.

Quick Thought, Decision and Action

One of the most valuable points of information about a prospect is in regard to quickness, or slowness of thought, decision and action.

People of this type are the most responsive, the quickest, the most impatient, the most practical of any type of people you meet.

These people *see* relationships, rather than reasoning them out slowly and elaborately.

With them to see is to think, to think is to conclude immediately, to conclude is to speak or to act. They want to be shown, they will believe their eyes more quickly than their ears.

They want facts. They want to know that the thing is practicable and useful. They do not want long explanations, long arguments, long descriptions, or long-continued pleadings.

Figure 20—Severe, Stern, Economical Type.

How to Appeal to This Man

This man is one of the easiest of all types to deal with when you understand his nature. He presents a severe and forbidding appearance, and seems strong and resistant. No frontal attack is likely to win—nor can you appeal to any of the softer, warmer, more human instincts or desires. He has his weaknesses, however, and they are great. One of these is caution. Another is fear of loss—loss of money, loss of reputation, loss of prestige. Do not threaten him, however, but show him how your proposition will safeguard him against loss.

Severe, Stern, Economical Type

Doubtless you have had the experience of meeting a person who looked very severe and cross only to find upon closer acquaintance that he was mild, gentle, good-natured, and rather easy-going. It is, therefore, worth while to learn to distinguish between those who are really hard-headed and stern and those who only appear to be.

Those who truly belong to this type have a high crown—that is, their heads are high, and square directly above the opening of the ears, but rather low and flat just above the temples and behind the forehead.

Their faces are long, their lips are thin and tightly compressed, the upper one being long and rather stiff-looking.

Their chins are long and square, their eyes cold and rather expressionless, their skin is cold and pale, as also are their lips and hands.

These peoples' hands are square, with rather knotty joints in the fingers, square finger tips, with hard flesh and stiff joints.

The backs of their heads are short from the ears back, and flat—sometimes showing a straight line, in profile, from the crown down through the neck.

These people are not friendly, not easily impressed, stubborn and tenacious, independent, self-controlled, self-reliant, cautious, conservative, economical, rather taciturn and uncommunicative.

These people are not easily flattered, they demand facts, and are most powerfully appealed to through self-interest and their desire to make and to save money.

Figure 21—Easy-going, Impressionable, Extravagant Type.

How to Appeal to This Man

You may appeal to this man's desires for pleasure, profit, and superiority; to his sympathy, generosity, and good-nature; to his instinct for companionship; but you can make no very successful appeal to his sense of duty and responsibility or his caution.

Easy-Going, Impressionable, Extravagant Type

People of this type have a low, round crown; head high and dome-shaped above the temples and just back of the forehead; wide open eyes; full, curved, red lips, hanging rather loosely; curves and dimples in the cheeks and chin; round face; small, retreating chin; soft, pliable, warm, pink hands; a narrow head, full back-head, and a short upper lip.

These people are very impressionable, emotional, impulsive, fond of good things, inclined to be extravagant in their expenditures. They are usually good mixers, like people, like to be with them, and enjoy their companionship, are usually much interested in the opposite sex, and are inclined to be rather reckless and lacking in self-respect.

Figure 22—The Man Who Wants Facts.

How to Appeal to This Man

In all you say to this man, bear in mind that he wants to know exactly what you have to offer, what it is for, what it will do, what practical results he may expect, what it will cost, and when he can get it. Talk business every minute.

The Man Who Wants Facts

The typical man who wants facts, who demands to be shown, and who refuses to be moved by mere plausible theories, has a high, retreating forehead, with prominent brows, his hands and finger tips are square, and as a usual thing he is more likely to be blond than brunet, although people of this type who are brunet are also more inclined to want facts than theories.

Figure 23—The Who Wants Reasons.

How to Appeal to This Man

Men of this type are sometimes more influenced by an ingenious and attractive theory than by facts and figures. If the theory seems sound to them, they are willing to take the facts for granted. Their observation is not good and it is hard to hold them down to facts. They are usually imaginative, however, and can see clearly any mental picture you may paint.

The Man Who Wants Reasons

The man who wants reasons has a full, wide upper forehead, rather knotty finger joints, and is more likely to want reasons if he is a brunet than if he is a blond.

Figure 24—Responds Easily to Word of Command.

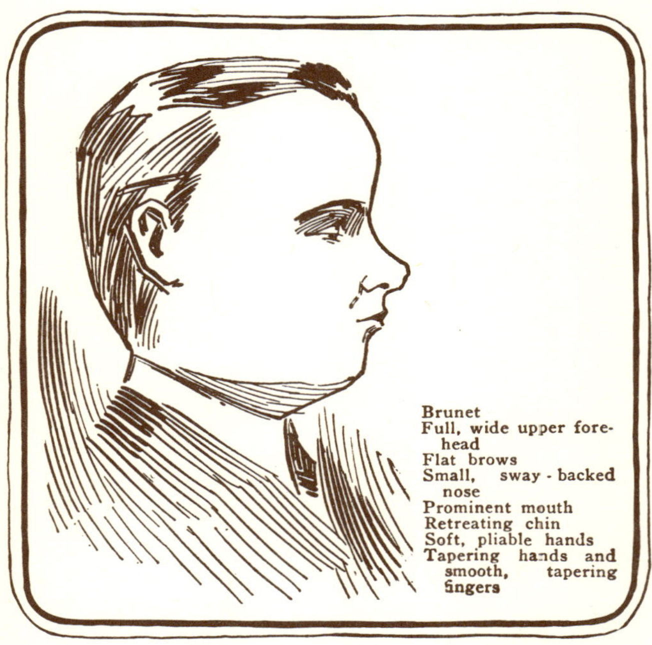

How to Appeal to This Man

Give him a beautiful theory, paint for him a vivid mental picture of himself enjoying your proposition, and then speak the direct Word of Command. Do not be too long about either your theory or your mental picture, because he is impulsive and impatient and acts quickly under the spur of emotion or in response to the Word of Command. The foregoing applies to the extreme type. You may have to give more moderate types more facts and more appeals to instincts and desires.

Respond Easily to Word of Command

The man who responds most easily to the Word of Command has a full, round, broad, upper forehead; flat brows; retroussé or sway-back nose; prominent mouth; a retreating chin; and soft, pliable, tapering hands and fingers.

Making the Combination

As you study the types shown and described in the preceding pages you will see at once that two or more sets of typical indications may be shown in any one individual.

For example, one man may have all the indications for an instinct for physical activity together with all of the indications of the instinct for companionship. It is easy enough to combine these instincts and to conclude that this individual not only likes activity but he likes activities with others. He is not the sort of man who will go off by himself on a bicycle trip, or a canoe trip, or a hunting or fishing trip, but he enjoys more social sports, such as golf, tennis, base-ball, bowling, billiards, or tramping parties.

In another man you may see all of the indications of a desire to make money, together with all of the indications of the desire to serve others. This is a very common type.

Such a man is not only interested in his business, which may be manufacturing, merchandising, or transportation, but is also interested in the welfare of his employees, in giving the very highest and best service to his customers, and perhaps also in philanthropy, benevolence or some form of social uplift.

How to Determine Degree of Intensity of an Instinct or Desire

You notice that a number of different indications were given for every instinct, desire or type.

As you looked around you at your relatives and acquaintances, you discovered that most of them had some of the indications of almost every one of the instincts or desires. The question naturally arose in your mind which of these is stronger, or strongest.

The rules to follow are simple:

First, any indication which shows itself in marked degree—as for example, extreme high-headedness, extreme wide-headedness—must be given more consideration than any indication which appears in only a moderate degree.

Second, the more indications of any instinct or desire you observe in any one individual the stronger will that instinct or desire be.

For example, if a man is blond, high-headed, wide-headed, has the type of face which indicates great quickness of thought, decision, speech and action; has square shoulders, square hands, and large bones and muscles, he is very much more active physically than a man who is only blond and wide-headed but has a narrow, tapering chin.

This will serve as a warning to you that you must never base your final judgment of a man upon any one indication alone.

When you observe a man and see an indication of the instinct for mental activity, or the instinct for possession, look for the other indications. Verify. Check up. See how many indications he has of the instinct or desire, and how extreme each one is.

Go Slowly at First.—You will find it necessary to proceed rather slowly at first in applying the knowledge gained in this lesson. Reason carefully to your conclusions.

The more practice you have, however, the more you train your observation, the more you verify your conclusions by observing the individual in action, the more rapidly and accurately will you be able to observe and the more quickly and easily you will be able to arrive at your conclusions. Finally you will be able to size up your prospect in regard to his leading instincts and desires as easily as you would read a page in a book.

SUMMARY

Points to Remember in This Lesson

Perhaps the most helpful way to sum up this instruction will be to list the various outward indications of inward characteristics in certain groups.

Some people are quick, keen, alert, positive, dynamic, active, decisive, eager, enthusiastic, ambitious, and courageous. Let us call this the positive type.

Other people are slow, mild, meditative, negative, static, quiet, deliberate, calm, phlegmatic, unambitious, cautious, and conservative. Let us call this the negative type.

And these are the indications:

Positive	*Negative*
Blond color	Brunet color
Retreating forehead	Full forehead
Prominent brows	Flat brows
Prominent eyes	Deep-set eyes
Large, prominent nose	Small or sway-backed nose
Prominent mouth	Retreating mouth
Retreating chin	Prominent chin
Medium or small size	Large size
Fine hair, skin, and features	Coarse hair, skin, and features
Hard or elastic hands	Soft hands
Pliable hands	Stiff hands
Square jaw	Round jaw
Square shoulders	Sloping shoulders
Large bones and muscles	Much fat on frame
High, wide, short, round head	Low, narrow, long, square head
Alert, keen expression	Dull, calm expression
Buoyant health	Moderate health

There are here twenty indications of positiveness and twenty negative—counting the four head-types.

You will see few people who have all the positive indications—and few who have all the negative indications. The value of the list lies in the fact that the more positive indications a man shows the more positive he is—the more negative indications, the more negative.

Exercises

1. Analyze yourself according to the indications for the instincts by studying yourself in a mirror and writing down the indications for each of the instincts in turn.

For example, suppose you are blond; with high, narrow head; high cheek bones; high-bridged nose; square jaw; fairly broad, square shoulders; medium chest; rather slender bones and muscles; medium-sized, rather tapering hands and fingers; elastic and flexible hands, and medium-sized feet. Checking this over, you find seven positive indications of instinct for physical activity; four "medium" indications of it; and four negative indications, as follows:

Positive

1. Blond
2. High head
3. High cheek bones
4. High-bridged nose
5. Square jaw
6. Elastic hands
7. Flexible hands

Medium

1. Fairly broad, square shoulders
2. Medium chest
3. Medium-sized hands
4. Medium-sized feet

Negative

1. Narrow head
2. Slender bones
3. Slender muscles
4. Tapering hands and fingers

Positive

To average these indications is easy:

Seven positive count one each........	7
Four "medium" count one-half each..	2
Total	9

Negative

Four negative count one each........	4
Four "medium" count one-half each...	2
Total	6

Total number of points 15, 9 showing for physical activity, 6 against it; percentage in favor $9 \div 15 = 60\%$.

2. The first exercise should show you which of the instincts has the highest percentage of indications. Now refer to your experience. Is this your strongest instinct? The one which responds most readily to appeal? If you honestly think not, go back over your figures and see whether or not some indications may be so marked that you should give them one and one-half or two points instead of one.

3. Follow the same method in analyzing yourself as to desires, and check up your experience to find whether or not you have reached correct conclusions.

4. Analyze as many of your relatives and friends in the same way, checking up carefully in each case to determine how nearly accurate your analysis is.